Brixworth

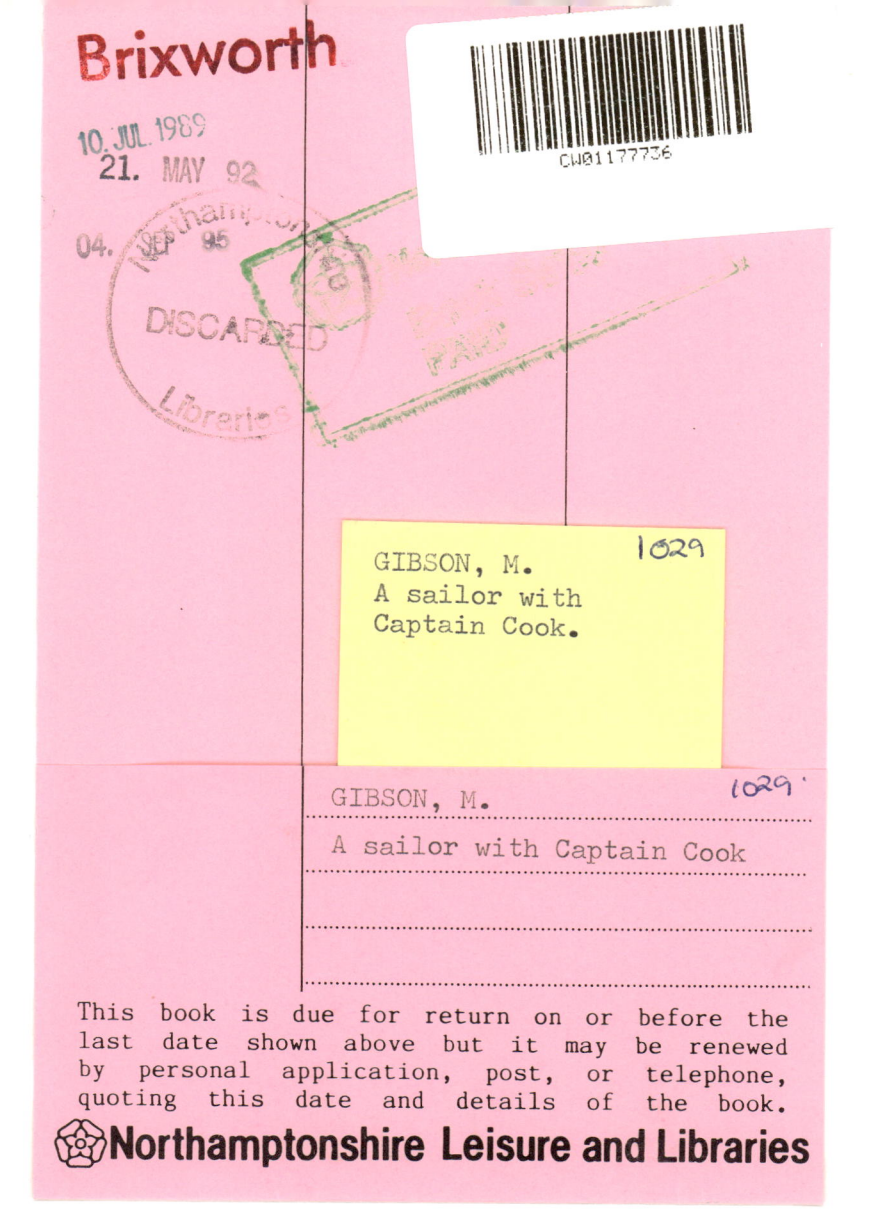

10. JUL. 1989
21. MAY 92
04. SEP 95

DISCARDED

GIBSON, M.   1029
A sailor with
Captain Cook.

GIBSON, M.   1029
A sailor with Captain Cook

This book is due for return on or before the last date shown above but it may be renewed by personal application, post, or telephone, quoting this date and details of the book.

Northamptonshire Leisure and Libraries

00 300 091 029

HOW THEY LIVED

A SAILOR WITH CAPTAIN COOK

MICHAEL GIBSON

Illustrated by
Mark Bergin

HOW THEY LIVED

An American Pioneer Family
An Aztec Warrior
A Celtic Family
A Child in Victorian London
A Colonial American Merchant
A Crusading Knight
An Edwardian Household
A Family in the Fifties
A Family in World War I
A Family in World War II
An Ice Age Hunter
An Inca Farmer
A Medieval Monk
A Medieval Serf

A Norman Baron
A Plains Indian Warrior
A Plantation Slave
A Roman Centurion
A Sailor with Captain Cook
A Samurai Warrior
A Saxon Farmer
A Slave in Ancient Greece
A Soldier in Wellington's Army
A Teenager in the Sixties
A Tudor Merchant
A Victorian Factory Worker
A Viking Sailor

Editor: Amanda Earl

First published in 1987 by
Wayland (Publishers) Limited
61 Western Road, Hove
East Sussex BN3 1JD, England

© Copyright 1987 Wayland (Publishers) Limited

British Library Cataloguing in Publication Data
Gibson, Michael, *1936*–
A sailor with Captain Cook. – (How they lived)
1. Seafaring life – History – 18th
century – Juvenile literature 2. Sailing
ships – History – 18th century – Juvenile literature
1. Title   II. Bergin, Mark   III. Series
359.1'09'033   G540

ISBN 0 85078 735 1

Typeset by Kalligraphics Limited, Redhill, Surrey
Printed and bound in Belgium by Casterman S.A.

CONTENTS

THE STORM 4

THE ENDEAVOUR 6

THE OFFICERS 8

RECRUITING 10

A SAILOR'S LIFE 12

ON BOARD SHIP 14

NAVIGATION 16

DEFENCE AND THE MARINES 18

FOOD AND DRINK 20

DEATH AND DISEASE 22

DISCIPLINE AND PUNISHMENT 24

GAMES AND AMUSEMENTS 26

DANGERS AT SEA 28

JOURNEY'S END 30

GLOSSARY 31

MORE BOOKS TO READ 31

INDEX 32

The Storm

The mountainous seas crashed down on the little ship drenching it with bitterly cold spray. Gale force winds tilted the vessel so much that one side, then the other, was nearly under water.

Sixteen-year-old Isaac Smith wished he had never been born. He had been sick, so sick, for hours. He began to curse the day his parents had persuaded his cousin, James Cook, to take him on as a member of the crew of H.M.S. *Endeavour*.

The rigging and ship's timbers creaked and moaned as if they were about to be torn apart. Isaac groaned and was sick again . . .

Gradually, however, the storm blew itself out and the *Endeavour* stopped leaping and twisting and returned little by little to its normal rolling motion. Isaac breathed a sigh of relief. 'Move yourself, you lazy landlubber,' roared the bosun. Isaac jumped up and set to work again, all other worries forgotten.

Isaac was on a Royal Navy expedition headed by James Cook, which was to last from 1768 to 1771. The purpose of the expedition was to observe the passage of the planet Venus across the skies above the island of Tahiti, and to search for the Great Southern Continent which

no European had ever seen.

Cook was one of the finest navigators of all time and Isaac Smith was, in some ways, a very fortunate young man to be able to accompany him on his first great voyage.

On their three-year voyage, the crew of the Endeavour *faced many terrible storms in the small sailing ship.*

THE ENDEAVOUR

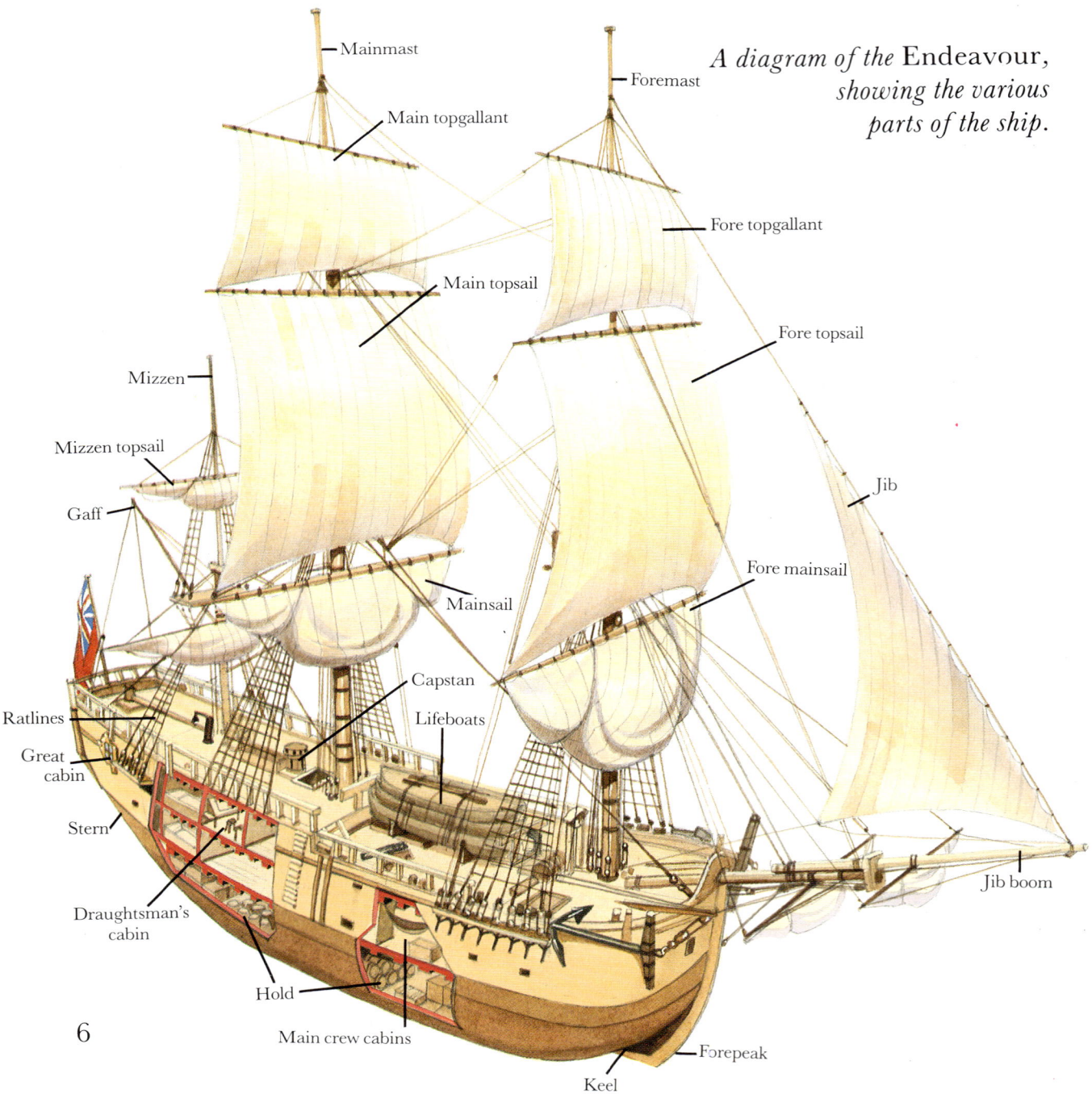

A *diagram of the* Endeavour, *showing the various parts of the ship.*

For the great expedition, Cook and his crew travelled in a small sailing ship called the *Endeavour*. It was only 35m long, 10m across at its widest point and about 4m in depth. This tiny ship weighed 386 tonnes and carried a company of 94 men.

The *Endeavour* was made of a skeleton of tough beams covered with wooden planks. Bits of old rope called 'oakum' were packed between the planks and covered with melted pitch to make the hull watertight. The *Endeavour* had three masts – the fore, main and mizzen. The main mast was over 30m high.

The masts were supported by a network of ropes called stays and shrouds. The shrouds were made into rope ladders by fastening ratlines across them. The sailors had to run up the ratlines to set up, take in or furl the sails. The ship was guided through the water by a helmsman who pushed the huge wooden rudder from side to side.

In harbour, the *Endeavour* was kept in position by two huge anchors which were dropped over the side and lodged in the seabed.

In this tiny ship, Cook and his crew were to sail around the world.

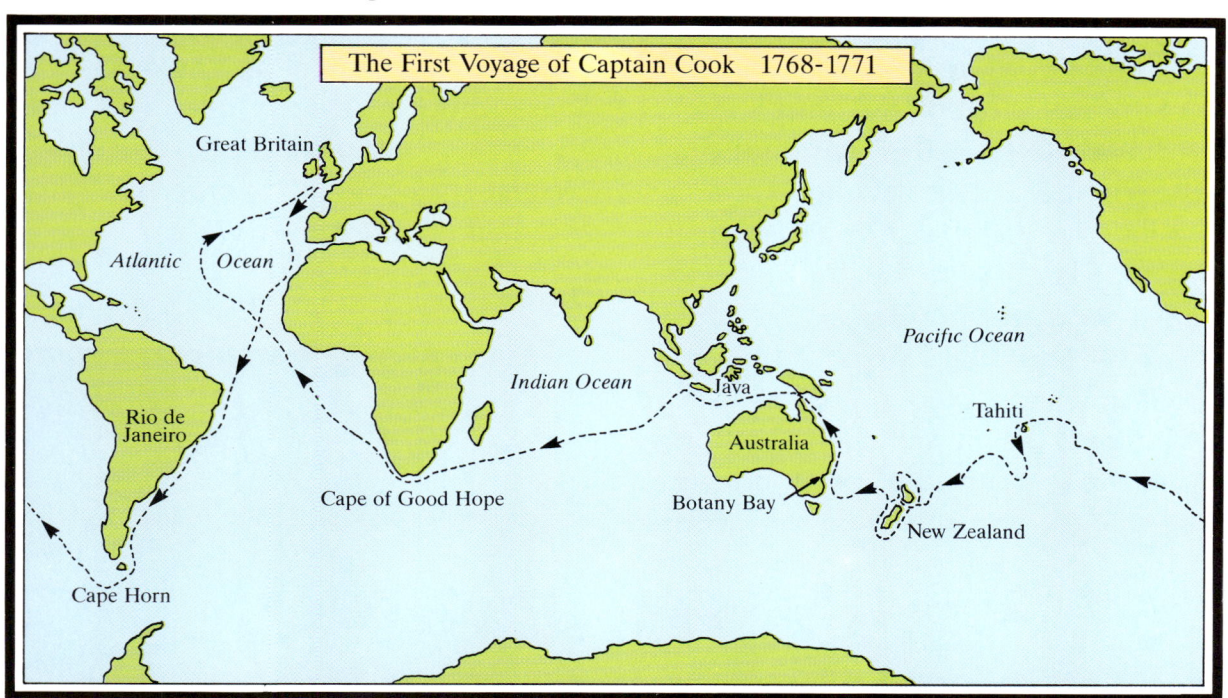

The Officers

Officers played a vital role in the running of the *Endeavour*. As Cook's sailors worked so hard in unpleasant overcrowded conditions, fights and upsets were common. It was up to the officers on board, and finally the captain himself to make sure everything ran smoothly.

Royal Navy officers were a special breed. They joined as midshipmen. After six years they were allowed to take their lieutenant's examination. If they passed, they received what was known as a commission, and became full officers. Although every lieutenant dreamed of commanding his own ship, few ever did.

The captain of a ship had enormous powers. Some captains were monsters, hated and feared by all the crew. Others, like James Cook, were loved and respected.

Beneath the commissioned officers came the warrant and petty officers. The master was the most important warrant officer as he was responsible for navigating the ship. The surgeon on board ship was also a warrant officer, who treated the men's illnesses and wounds.

The gunner was an important petty officer who looked after the cannon, ammunition and gunpowder. Other petty officers also had their own special jobs. The armourer looked after the ship's muskets, pistols and cutlasses. The carpenter plugged leaks and made good any damage to the ship's fabric. The sailmaker patched old sails and made new ones when necessary. The bosun took charge of the stores and set the crew to work. The quartermasters steered the ship. The cook was the least important petty officer.

Right *It was the duty of officers to make sure that the ship ran smoothly.*

Below *Cook was a respected captain.*

RECRUITING

The *Endeavour* had a crew of thirty-nine able seamen aged between 16 and 45 years of age. With pay at less than a pound a month, there were not many volunteers.

Many sailors were actually 'press-ganged' into service. Squads of marines were sent to tour the local public houses and round up any suitable men. Drunken men were often

The crews of some ships 'press-ganged' men into service.

Before joining a ship's crew, many sailors had been tramps or criminals. This cartoon of 1808 depicts some 'rough-and-ready' sailors.

bundled away before they knew what was happening to them. More troublesome customers were knocked on the head and carried unconscious on board ship.

Magistrates working in courts close to the ports gave tramps, smugglers and criminals the choice of joining the Navy or going to prison.

In addition to these unwilling sailors, there were a few volunteers like Isaac Smith. Some captains attracted volunteers by their fame. Captains also marched around the ports making speeches and tempting their listeners with rum, in the hope that they might join the ship's company.

In wartime, many men joined the Navy to win what was known as 'prize money'. A captured enemy ship would be sold and each member of the victorious crew would be given a share of the profits.

Finally, many charities and workhouses supplied the Navy with orphans and abandoned boys. No matter what they had been before they joined their ships, the Navy expected to turn them into 'true hearts of oak' after a few weeks at sea!

Homeless boys and orphans often became cabin boys on board Royal Navy ships. This eighteenth-century drawing shows one such cabin boy.

A Sailor's Life

Conditions on board ship were appalling. There was little room. The men slept jammed side by side in hammocks in the dark, dank, smelly 'between deck' areas. There were no toilets or washing facilities. The sailors had to use the ship's scuppers (drainage holes). Soap was

Sailors lived in terrible conditions. Their 'mess' room was dark, filthy and overcrowded.

not issued until 1810 and even then the men were made to pay for it.

The sailors lived together in a room or 'mess', where they ate their food during rest periods, chatted, sang or told stories. At the centre of each mess there was a table which hung from hooks set into the ceiling. It was very important that all the members of a mess got on well. Difficult sailors were moved on from one mess to another. Really unpleasant men often had a mess on their own.

The seamen were divided into groups of 'watches' or working parties. A watch usually lasted for four hours. On most ships, men were expected to work 'watch and watch', that is, to work one watch and then rest the next. Captain Cook was a careful commander and only required his men to work for one watch while resting for two.

The situation on board Royal Navy ships was often explosive. If the officers were brutal, crews rose up in mutiny and tried to overthrow them. If there were troublemakers among the crew, fights were common, some leading to deaths. It is a tribute to Cook's skill that the *Endeavour's* three-year voyage around the world passed without any serious disturbances.

Sometimes conditions on board Navy ships became so bad that sailors rose up in mutiny. A famous example was on the HMS Bounty, *when Captain Bligh's crew mutinied against his brutal rule.*

ON BOARD SHIP

'All hands on deck! Ahoy! Do you hear the news there below? Come up every man and mother's son of you.' At five o'clock every morning, the roaring voice of the bosun's mate woke the crew for their watch and sent them rushing up on deck. For two hours they worked hard in the cold light of dawn. At about eight o'clock, cabin boys brought the sailors their breakfast. It was usually *burgoo*, a mixture of porridge and chopped meat, and 'Scotch Coffee' made from burnt ship's biscuits and boiling water. As soon as they had gobbled their food, they were back hard at work.

On Mondays, the crew carried out arms drill with muskets and cutlasses. On Tuesdays, they did boat drill: the ship's lifeboats were lowered into the sea and hauled out again time after time to make sure that it could be done quickly in an emergency. On Wednesdays, they practised shortening the sails (reefing) by rolling up the ends and tying them in place with laces. The sails were also furled; that is, they were tied to the poles as if the ship was preparing for a storm.

Thursdays were 'make-and-mend' days when all the minor repairs on the ship were done. On Fridays, the men practised running out the cannon and firing them as fast as they could. On Saturdays, the ship's decks were scrubbed with pieces of sandstone called 'holystones' until they shone. The decks were then sanded to make them less slippery for the sailors.

Although Sundays were rest days, the captain inspected the whole ship's company to make sure they were fit, clean and properly dressed. After that he read the Morning Service from a Prayer Book and the crew sung hymns they had learned by heart. The rest of the day was free, yet there was little to do to pass the time. A sailor's life was hard and monotonous.

Captain Cook believed that the best way to avoid fights and arguments among his crew, was to keep the sailors busy. The first 'watch' started at 5 o'clock in the morning. Each day there were special jobs to complete, such as furling the sails, and making minor repairs to the ship.

NAVIGATION

Finding your way around the oceans of the world in the eighteenth century was no easy task. Although navigators had compasses to help them set course in any direction they wanted to go, it was still difficult.

On leaving port, the master of the ship had to be able to estimate the ship's latitude – the position north or south of the Equator.

This was calculated by measuring the angle between the sun and the horizon with a quadrant and checking this in special tables. Longitude, movement west or east, was worked out with the help of a very accurate clock called a *chronometer*. This showed the time at 0° longitude – the Greenwich meridian. (It was called this as it was on the site of the Royal Observatory at Greenwich). With the help of a sextant and a book of tables, the master was able to work out local time wherever he was. By calculating the difference between Greenwich time and local time, the master was able to work out his exact longitude.

Sailing along unknown, unmapped coasts was extremely dangerous. A specially qualified sailor was placed in the bow of the ship. From time to time, he threw a line weighted with lead into the sea to measure its depth. In this way, the master avoided patches of shallow water and reefs of jagged rocks which could rip out the ship's bottom.

Navigation required great skill and knowledge and, in unknown waters, plenty of luck.

Below *Instruments used by Cook and his officers to aid navigation.*

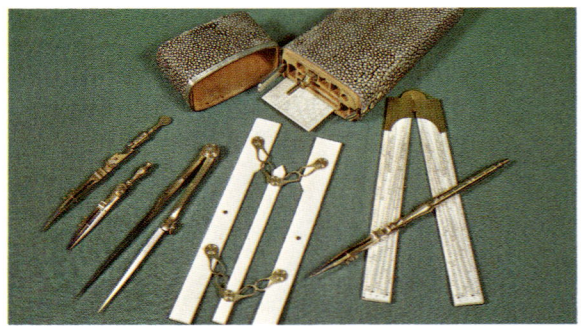

Below *With the help of a sextant, the crew could work out local time accurately.*

Cook takes a reading from a sextant while an officer writes notes. By working out the difference between Greenwich time and local time, the ships exact longitude position could be gained.

DEFENCE AND THE MARINES

The crew of the *Endeavour* included ten marines. These marines had a high opinion of themselves as they were paid more than the ordinary sailors and wore smart scarlet and white uniforms with tall black hats.

Marines were armed with muskets, an early form of rifle, and bayonets, a short sword which could be pushed on to the barrel of the musket. Muskets with fixed bayonets were used like stabbing spears to

Sailors are instructed by marines to secure the cannon during a heavy storm.

could be pointed in any direction.

In times of danger, a gun was loaded by ramming a gunpowder cartridge, a cannon-ball and a wad of stuffing down the barrel. Fine powder was then poured into a touchhole which was connected by a narrow channel to the barrel. When this powder was set alight, the flame ran down the channel and set fire to the cartridge. When the cartridge exploded the cannon-ball was forced out of the barrel with great force.

Although the *Endeavour* was a tiny ship it was able to defend itself.

A model of the ship Endeavour. *Although only 35m long, the ship was equipped to defend itself, with 10 cannon and 12 swivel guns.*

Sailors practise positioning the cannon, for in unknown territory, it was important that Navy ships could defend themselves.

protect the crew in times of danger.

The *Endeavour* had 10 cannon and 12 swivel guns to help protect it. The cannon were placed on wheeled carriages so that they could be moved easily. The carriages were attached to the ship's side by chains and ropes. This stopped them rolling around in rough weather and damaging the ship. Swivel guns were smaller and mounted on the ship's side so they

19

FOOD AND DRINK

If a voyage was to be successful, it was important for the sailors to stay healthy. Before leaving Plymouth, Cook was ordered to make every effort to keep his crew fit. When the *Endeavour* set sail, it was like Noah's Ark, full of sheep, pigs and hens, to provide the sailors with fresh meat on their long journey. It also carried blocks of dried soup as well as 9,600kg of bread and 4,000kg of bread flour. In addition, there were 4,000 pieces of beef and 6,000 pieces of pork as well as 3,500kg of pickled cabbage and 187 bushels of peas.

On board ship, food quickly went bad. The bread became full of large, black-headed maggots while the

ship's biscuits became infested with pale, wriggly beatles called weevils. The men joked about having 'meat' with their bread and biscuit! Sailors quickly learnt to shake their food before eating it so that unwanted 'visitors' fell out.

The *Endeavour* carried 5,400l of beer and 7,300l of rum as well as lots of water. The water quickly became foul and stinking. The beer became so bad that the sailors had to hold their noses when they drank it.

Sailors loved their 'grog' or rum and got drunk whenever they had the chance. Overdrinking sometimes led to tragedies. Two of the ship's servants got drunk when visiting Tierra del Fuego, on the southern tip of South America, and fell asleep on the frozen ground. They died of exposure. Another sailor died after drinking a complete bottle of rum!

Sailors load the Endeavour *with food supplies for the long voyage.*

DEATH AND DISEASE

In the eighteenth century, disease and death were common on board Royal Navy ships. Sailors suffered from such illnesses as 'bloody flux', 'black vomit', 'dry belly-ache' and, worst of all, 'scurvy'. The symptoms of scurvy were 'large spots covering the whole surface of the body,

The surgeon's assistant gives the sailors a drink called 'wort' to try and safeguard against the disease 'scurvy'.

swollen legs, putrid gums and extreme tiredness'. This dreadful disease was caused by lack of vitamin C.

Although sailors knew nothing about vitamins, they learned from experience that crews remained healthy as long as they had fresh fruit and vegetables. So the surgeon dosed any sailor who looked as if he was sickening for scurvy with 'wort', a drink rich in malt. Another safeguard against the disease was to eat pickled cabbage. At first, the men did not want to eat this strange vegetable, so Cook reserved its use for the officers who pretended it was a great delicacy. Soon, the sailors were

Cook and his crew visited many unusual and faraway countries. The sailors remained healthy until they reached Java when several men fell ill.

only too keen to have their share.

As far as their journey to Batavia in Java, the health of the crew was remarkably good. But, while in harbour here, some sailors caught malaria and dysentery. The surgeon of the ship, and four sailors died and there were 40 men on the sick list on the voyage to Cape Town in South Africa. Between January and February 1771, many more sailors died and the journey came to a sad end.

23

DISCIPLINE AND PUNISHMENT

Discipline was harsh on Royal Navy ships. In the overcrowded conditions, quarrels and disobedience were common. Such crimes were unmercifully punished by flogging. The wrongdoer was tied to the main mast or the rigging and whipped with a cat-o'-nine-tails until his back was covered in cuts and blood. Salt was then rubbed into the wounds to stop poisoning. The pain was excruciating.

On 16 September 1768, a sailor and a marine were each given 12 lashes for refusing to eat their allowance of fresh beef. Sometimes, the mere thought of punishment was enough to cause a tragedy. When a marine called William Greenslade, was accused of stealing a piece of sealskin, he dived overboard and drowned himself rather than be disgraced. Yet some terrible accidents did happen on the *Endeavour*, and it proved that discipline was a necessary evil to prevent mistakes.

Sometimes, really cruel things happened on board ship. At one point during the voyage someone crept into the cabin of Cook's clerk, and cut off parts of his ears. Although Cook could not obtain definite proof, he was sure that two midshipmen were responsible and reduced both to the rank of able seamen.

Yet Cook was a merciful man. He knew that the best way of maintaining good discipline was by keeping his men hard at work rather than punishing them.

Left *Accidents could easily happen on board ship, so discipline was severe.*

Right *Disobedient sailors were brutally punished by flogging.*

24

GAMES AND AMUSEMENTS

Small Navy ships like the *Endeavour* could not offer crews much in the way of entertainment. Most of the time the sailors were kept hard at work and out of mischief. During fine weather, however, there were times when the men had little work to do, and needed to be amused. On these occasions, Cook organized team games between the different watches. The seamen would compete with each other to see who could trim the sails or run out and fire a cannon the fastest. The prize was usually an extra allowance of 'grog'.

At other times, teams of sailors raced each other up and down the rigging of the main mast. Sometimes, watches danced the 'hornpipe' on the main deck to the music of fiddles and pipes. The sailors would dance on the spot, miming the movements made when climbing the rope ladders.

Story-telling was also popular. One of the *Endeavour's* crew, Francis Haite, had sailed all over the world and told the most marvellous tales about his adventures. Many an hour was passed away listening to his stories.

Sometimes, there were special ceremonies on board ship, like that to mark the crossing of the Equator. Sailors who had not done this before were swung over the ship's side on ropes and ducked in the sea. Cook himself escaped this frightening experience by paying a fine, but 21 men and boys were 'ducked' on that occasion.

Right *Sailors did enjoy themselves sometimes. Here, a sailor dances the 'hornpipe' to music.*

Below *Some sailors made sketches of the strange animals they saw on the voyage.*

DANGERS AT SEA

Long sea voyages were filled with danger. A sudden squall could capsize a ship while uncharted reefs could rip out its bottom. On only its third day at sea, the *Endeavour* hit a violent gale and the main mast was damaged.

The Endeavour *reaches Funchal, the capital of Madeira, to get food supplies and water. It was at this port of call that a master's mate was killed in an accident as he helped to move the ship's anchor.*

The crew leave the Endeavour *as it flounders on a reef off the coast of Australia.*

Sailors got used to the accidents that happened at sea. Off Madeira, a master's mate, was killed helping to move the anchor. He became tangled in the guide rope and was dragged to the bottom of the sea.

For smooth sailing, it was important to keep the *Endeavour* in good condition at all times. As the voyage went on, the underneath of the ship

became covered in a mass of barnacles and weeds. It was the sailors' job to remove them. By steering the ship into a shallow cove, and moving all the stores on board to one side, the ship tilted enough to enable the sailors to clean the underside. First, the weeds and barnacles were burnt off. Then, the hull was scraped clean and 'caulked', that is, the gaps between the planks were filled with oakum and painted with pitch.

Later, off the east coast of

Sailors start to repair the large hole ripped in the Endeavour's *hull after hitting a hidden coral reef while navigating the Australian coastline. Only by tilting the ship to one side could the repair work begin.*

Australia, the *Endeavour* ran aground on a hidden coral reef. To get the ship off guns and decayed stores had to be thrown overboard. Lightened in this way, sailors were able to haul the *Endeavour* free.

Journey's End

On 13th July 1771, the *Endeavour* finally anchored in England after a voyage of three years. Although 38 of the original crew of 94 men had died, the voyage had been a great success. The entire coastline of New Zealand and the east coast of Australia had been explored and mapped. The passage of the planet Venus had been observed and a huge collection of plant and animal specimens had been made.

Many sailors were sad that the voyage and the adventure was over. On receiving their wages, they made their way quietly home. After a rest, many sailors were drawn back to the sea with all its dangers, excitement and hard work. Some of these men perished in the wars which were soon to break out. Other sailors stayed safely at home, where they boasted of their exciting adventures on the good ship *Endeavour*.

Although from a later voyage, this picture is an example of the beautiful places Cook's sailors visited.

GLOSSARY

Bosun Officer in charge of the sails and rigging. His duties also included rousing the men for their duty.

Bushel An old-fashioned measure (approximately 36l) for fruit, grain, and peas.

Compass An instrument with a magnetic needle, which is used to find direction.

Cutlass A short sword with a slightly curved blade used by sailors.

Dysentery An infectious disease causing very bad diarrhoea.

Equator An imaginary line making a circle around the earth halfway between the North and South Poles.

Furl To roll up and bind a sail.

Galley The ship's kitchen.

Greenwich meridian One of the imaginary lines (0° degrees longitude) which run at right angles to the Equator.

Grog The seamen's allowance of rum.

Helmsman The sailor who steers the ship.

Hold The space at the bottom of the ship for storing cargo.

Latitude The distance of a place north or south of the Equator. It is measured in degrees, 1 degree representing about 110km.

Longitude The distance of a place east or west of the Greenwich meridian.

Malaria A fever caused by a tiny parasite, carried by mosquitos.

Mate A First Officer on a merchant ship.

Midshipman A young man training to be a naval officer.

Oakum Loose fibres made by picking old rope into pieces.

Pitch A thick, black substance made from coal tar, which is liquid when hot and hardens when left to cool.

Ratline A short rope fastened across two shrouds like ladder rungs.

Rigging The ropes, sails and stays of a ship.

Sextant An instrument for measuring the height of stars, used to aid navigation.

Southern Continent From early times, people believed that there had to be a great continent in the South Seas to balance the northern continents of Europe, Asia and Africa.

Scuppers Holes in a ship's side to carry off water from the deck.

Shrouds A set of ropes forming the rigging for the masts.

Squall A strong and sudden gust of wind, usually followed by heavy rain.

MORE BOOKS TO READ

Alan Blackwood, *Captain Cook*, (Wayland, 1986).

Gian Paolo Ceserani, *The Travels of Captain Cook*, (Kestrel, 1979).

Tom Jauncey, *Great Explorers*, (Wayland, 1986).

Sheila Lewenhak, *The voyages of Captain Cook*, (Longman, 1978).

Kathleen Monham, *Famous names in Seafaring*, (Wayland, 1980).

David Sylvester, *Captain Cook and the Pacific*, (Longman, 1971).

INDEX

Accidents 21, 24, 28
Australia 29, 30

Bosun, the 4, 8, 14

Cabin boys 11, 14
Cape Town 23
Chronometer 16
Compasses 16
Cook, Captain 4, 5, 7, 8, 13, 23, 24, 26
Coral reefs 16, 28, 29
Criminals 11

Defence 8, 14, 18–19
Discipline 24
Diseases 22–23

Endeavour, the 4, 5, 6–7, 8, 13, 18, 19, 20, 26, 28, 29, 30
Equator, the 6, 26
Expedition 7
  purpose of 4, 30

Food and drink 13, 14, 20–21

Games and entertainment 26–27

Health and fitness 20, 23
Helmsman 7
'Hornpipe', the 26

Java 23

Latitude and longitude 16–17
Living conditions 8, 12–13, 24

Madeira 28
Marines 10, 18–19
Mutiny 13

Navigation 5, 8, 16–17
New Zealand 30

Officers 8–9, 23
Orphans 11

'Press-gangs' 10
'Prize money' 11
Punishment 24

Recruiting 10–11
Religion 14
Repairs 14, 29
Royal Navy 4, 8, 11, 13, 22, 24
Royal Observatory 16

Sailors 10, 11, 13, 16, 18, 23, 24, 30
  work 7, 8, 14, 26
  'watches' 13, 14, 26
'Scurvy' 22–23
Sextant 16
Storms 4–5, 14
Surgeon, ship's 8, 23

Tahiti 4
Tierra del Fuego 21

Venus 4, 30
Volunteers 10, 11
Voyage, the 20, 23, 28, 30

Wartime 11, 30

Picture acknowledgements
The pictures in this book were supplied by the following: BBC Hulton Picture Library 11 (left); The Fotomas Index 29; John Freeman & Co. 26; The Mansell Collection 13 (right), 28 (right); Mary Evans Picture Library 23; Michael Holford 16 (both), 19 (right); National Maritime Museum 11 (right), 30; TOPHAM 8. The artwork on page 8 is by Malcolm S. Walker. All remaining pictures are from the Wayland Picture Library.